FINISHING SCHOOL

FINISHING SCHOOL

Understanding and perfecting the most neglected stage of the golf swing

Steve Gould and D. J. Wilkinson

Foreword by Juli Inkster

First published 2016 by
Elliott and Thompson Limited
27 John Street, London WC1N 2BX
www.eandtbooks.com

ISBN: 978-1-78396-289-1

Competition photographs © Charles Briscoe-Knight
Photographs on pages 19, 218, 219, 221, 224 courtesy of the
Knightsbridge Golf School
Photographs on page 222 by Mark Barton

9 8 7 6 5 4 3 2 1

A catalogue record for this book is available from the British Library.

Designed by Jon Wainwright

Printed and bound in Italy by Printer Trento

Contents

We would like to thank:
Pippa Crane, Lorne Forsyth, Mark Barton,
Philip Talbot, Dave Lamplough, Chris Dale,
Charles Briscoe-Knight, Tony Lawrence, Grant
Richens, Henry Mendus, Robin Vaughan, Jon
Wainwright and Alison Menzies.

Foreword

I had already won two US Amateur Championships when, in 1981, my husband and teacher Brian first took me to London to see Leslie King. Brian wanted him to look at my swing and see what steps should be taken to lift my game to the next level.

I was fascinated when 'the old master' started honing my swing by primarily working on my finish. In particular he made me pay attention to the arc of the hands and arms through the post-impact position.

I spent most of my time practising his trademark Front End Therapy drill. Once happy with that, he then sculpted the rest of my swing into the finish, while making allowances for my individual swing mannerisms.

When we returned home Brian continued to work to Mr King's guidelines and I went on to win a further Amateur Championship. Then, as a professional, I won two US Opens and was later honoured to be elected to the World Golf Hall of Fame.

Looking at the swings of today's pros, on both the men's and ladies' tours, I'm amazed at how technically identical they are to the technique pioneered by Leslie King back in the late 1930s.

I'm pleased to see that the Knightsbridge Golf School is more successful than ever and that Dave and Steve have continued to develop and evolve Mr King's original teachings. I believe that *Finishing School* will prove to be a great help to all struggling golfers who have never realised how crucial building a sound post-impact arc is to building a consistent, repeatable golf swing.

Juli Inkster, seven-time Major championship winner

Introduction

Introduction

Over the last sixty-five years, the Knightsbridge Golf School has witnessed tens of thousands of golf swings, their owners ranging from the rawest of beginners to the most experienced of tour professionals.

During that time, golf instruction has developed from a few tips here and there into a hugely detailed industry, incorporating swing gurus, mental coaches, fitness programmes and much, much more.

It is fair to say that the set-up, backswing and downswing have now been well documented and in most cases well understood, to the point that the swing fundamentals of today's golfers are far superior to those of their predecessors.

What hasn't changed – and what has barely merited any focused attention – is what happens a nanosecond before impact, continuing through impact and into the follow-through. The finish, indeed, is widely regarded as an afterthought.

Yet it is vital to realise that what happens just after impact begins just before it, and so is crucial in determining the direction, distance and destination of the ball.

What so frustrates golfers is that they can hit five or six good shots in a row, followed by five or six bad ones, without perceptibly changing their swing. They don't know why this happens, or how to rectify it. They just know that this wretched sequence keeps repeating itself throughout their golfing lifetime. They are trapped in a perpetual, vicious circle.

Desperate for a solution, most trawl the Internet, study videos, take tips from golf magazines, tinker with their backswings or reroute their downswings. Sadly, nothing seems to make a difference. Why? It is simply because they are looking in the wrong place.

In the vast majority of cases the problem has nothing to do

with their set-up, backswing or downswing. It begins a split second before impact and reveals itself after impact and into the follow-through.

What these players should be doing is looking towards the finish, in order to help them sculpt a post-impact arc that is symmetrical to their pre-impact arc. The arc, after the ball has been struck, must be a carbon copy of what went before.

Once this has been established, the backswing and downswing can be blended into a consistent, defined, seamless and complete arc.

Like every other golf book, this one is designed to improve your game. More than that, though, we think it will completely change the way you think about the golf swing.

We want you to take a fresh look, and from a different angle. In effect, we want to teach you back-to-front. We want you to start at the finish.

We begin by looking at what we mean by keeping the arc symmetrical, and how that can be achieved. Once we understand the arc, we can move onto our programme for immediate improvement – we call it Front End Therapy – and highlight the finish by looking at it from overhead. To many golfers, these pictures could provide a light-bulb moment.

We then work backwards. We show how to deliver the club head powerfully and squarely into the ball, before returning to where we started and re-emphasising how the club's arc should be maintained through impact and into the finish.

You'll find in this book that we rely on pictures more than words to explain our technique. Experience has taught us that golfers learn far more from studying large, clearly labelled pictures than reading swathes of text. It may be a cliché but it is no less true – a picture really does paint a thousand words.

We also look at the same key points from a variety of

angles. Again, we have found that repetition of the same instruction, seen from different angles and described using different terms, often gets through to a reader who may have missed the point in its original form.

We see this frequently at the school when looking in on each other's lessons. Saying the same thing in a different way can produce that moment of enlightenment for our golfers. 'Why didn't you tell me that before?' is frequently the response.

You'll also find that the information here is supported by additional video content that you can find online at our website, www.knightsbridgegolfschool.com.

The teachings contained within this book are not theoretical. They have been proven in tens of thousands of lessons over the past sixty-five years since the Knightsbridge Golf School was founded. We are convinced that, by learning to build a post-impact, structured arc, we can finally bring to an end the miserable cycle of trial-and-error golf that you've been grappling with for so long.

The pictures opposite show real swings in motion. The pictures are not of a high quality – these are real golfers, not posed pictures – but the problem in each should still be easy to spot.

These golfers possess a more than serviceable backswing and downswing. In the split second before impact, however, the body stalls and the arms and hands pull the club head away from its intended arc through the impact area.

It is this movement that betrays itself in the distorted, contorted shapes seen here at impact and in the half-finish positions.

These players can and do hit some very good shots, but they are entirely dependent on the point and degree at which the club leaves the intended line.

If the club loses its arc a nanosecond after impact, the effects of the club being pulled in will go unnoticed, since the ball has already left the club.

But if the club loses its arc a nanosecond before impact, even by so much as a finger width, the shot is ruined.

This explains the inconsistencies of the struggling golfer. The only way he or she can make any permanent improvement is by learning how to keep the club on a constant arc, before and after impact.

'The follow-through and finish are integral parts of the swing which do not entirely look after themselves even though the backswing and downswing have been well carried out.

'The ball at impact spreads on the face of the club as it is compressed by the momentum of the club head at, and just after, impact. Therefore any deviation or impediment of the club head in the follow-through will affect the flight of the ball when it parts company with the club face.

'It is frequently claimed that the follow-through and finish reflect what has taken place earlier in the swing. True enough, up to a point, but many a shot has been ruined by a fault being allowed to creep in after impact.'

Leslie King, founder of the Knightsbridge Golf School, 1961

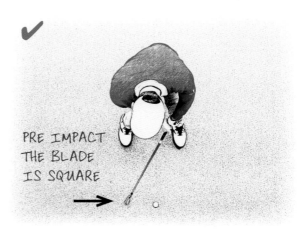

PRE IMPACT
THE BLADE
IS SQUARE

THE BLADE
IS SQUARE
AT IMPACT

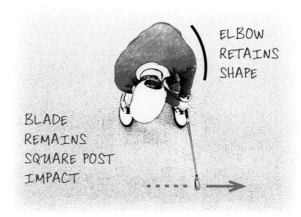

ELBOW
RETAINS
SHAPE

BLADE
REMAINS
SQUARE POST
IMPACT

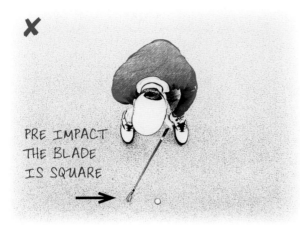

PRE IMPACT
THE BLADE
IS SQUARE

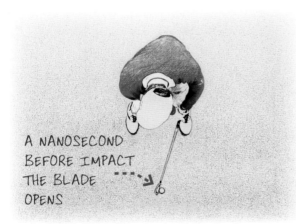

A NANOSECOND
BEFORE IMPACT
THE BLADE
OPENS

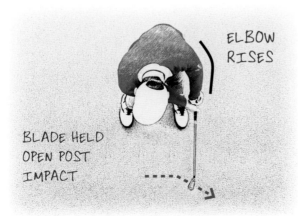

ELBOW
RISES

BLADE HELD
OPEN POST
IMPACT

An overhead view provides an instant visual reference to demonstrate the problem we will be addressing throughout this book.

In the top picture on both pages, the blade is square as it approaches impact. On the left side, the arc continues symmetrically, the elbow retains its shape, the blade is square at impact and post impact, and the ball leaves on the desired path.

In the right-hand sequence, a split second prior to impact the hands begin to cut in and the left elbow rises, leaving the club face open, which affects the path of the ball.

That is the purpose of this book: to demonstrate that even the slightest of movements in the nanosecond before or after impact can totally destroy an otherwise perfectly structured golf swing.

Understanding the Arc

Before we focus on building a model finish,
it is crucial to understand the concept of
the hand arc and its key role within the
golf swing. Great golf swings are built
around great hand arcs. Few golfers — or
their instructors — appreciate this.

Understanding the Arc

Throughout the impact zone, the hands and arms must maintain a constant radius from the body in order to keep the club on its own constant radius, and to keep it on a straight line while travelling from the few inches before impact to a few inches after.

To visualise this, imagine the bottom arc of two wheels: an inner wheel for the hands, which is followed by the right forefinger, and an outer wheel traced by the bottom of the club head.

Through the entire impact area, the hands must remain on the inner wheel to keep the club head on the outer wheel, which allows the ball to be driven powerfully and consistently forwards.

During a round of golf or a practice session a player might hit a number of good shots followed by a number of bad shots. Followed by more good shots and yet more bad shots. The player might well be perplexed by this variation, as it seems to him that nothing in his swing has changed.

The explanation is quite simple. The good shots happen when the hands pull in or rise up after impact and the effect goes unnoticed as the ball has already left the club face. However in the bad shots the hands pull in or rise up just before impact with catastrophic results for the path of the ball. It is for this reason that the post-impact arc is so important. It must be understood, learnt and incorporated into the swing.

So we have two arcs: a hand arc and a club head arc. The hand arc essentially, though not exclusively, dictates what happens to the club head arc (the component parts of the body also play a huge part in keeping the hands and club head on the inner and outer wheel but ultimately it is the hands that matter most).

The body can be moving in perfect unison but if the hands cut in, pull up or roll over through the impact zone, all the good work in the rest of the swing is pointless. This is why you might see swings that can look ugly and unconventional but produce outstanding results, while some swings that seem elegant and flowing end in disappointing results.

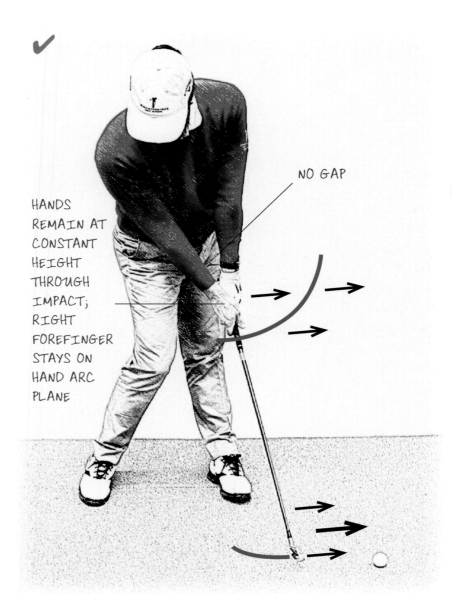

HANDS
REMAIN AT
CONSTANT
HEIGHT
THROUGH
IMPACT;
RIGHT
FOREFINGER
STAYS ON
HAND ARC
PLANE

NO GAP

The right forefinger stays on the inner wheel, ensuring that the club head stays on the outer wheel.

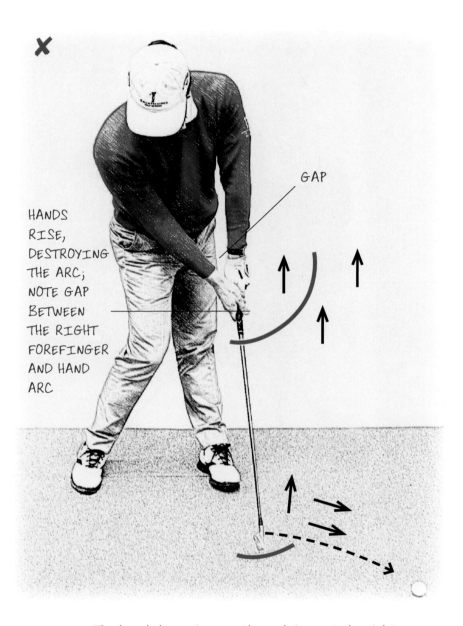

GAP

HANDS
RISE,
DESTROYING
THE ARC;
NOTE GAP
BETWEEN
THE RIGHT
FOREFINGER
AND HAND
ARC

The hands have risen up through impact; the right forefinger is well away from the inner wheel, the club head has risen up and moved away from the outer wheel.

NARROW GAP
BETWEEN LEFT
ARM AND BODY

RIGHT
FOREFINGER
STAYS ON
HAND ARC

CLUB HEAD
REMAINS ON
OUTER WHEEL

GAP HAS
INCREASED

HANDS
HAVE
RISEN

CLUB HEAD HAS CONTINUED
TO RISE THROUGH IMPACT,
AWAY FROM OUTER WHEEL

Here are those pictures again, side by side, so you can
clearly see that the hands have stayed on the inner
wheel, ensuring the club head stays on the outer wheel.

And here you can see that just a small lift in the first picture has had a greater effect on the later position; the hands have risen up from the inner wheel lifting the club head up and away from the outer wheel.

NO GAP
BETWEEN
ARMS

CLUB FACE SQUARE

In this sequence, the hands follow a perfect path; they do not twist or roll. The swing radius – the distance from the centre of the chest to the club head – is constant. The club head stays square to the body and follows its ideal arc. The ball comes out of the middle of the club face.

GAP
BETWEEN
ARMS
APPEARS
AS HANDS
CUT IN

CLUB FACE OPENS

In this second sequence, the hands and arms pull up during impact. You can see the start of a dreaded chicken wing: the left arm breaking at the elbow, disconnecting from the chest, the hands forced off their arc and holding the club face open. This shot will head way right.

Finishing School

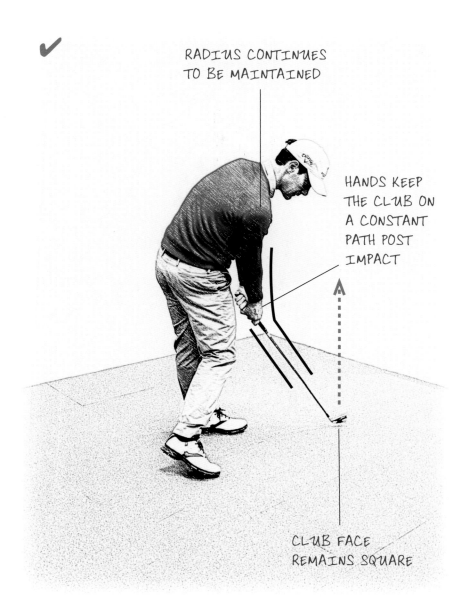

RADIUS CONTINUES
TO BE MAINTAINED

HANDS KEEP
THE CLUB ON
A CONSTANT
PATH POST
IMPACT

CLUB FACE
REMAINS SQUARE

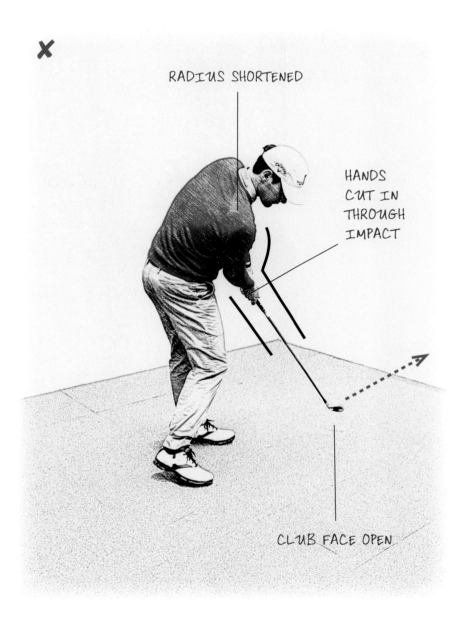

RADIUS SHORTENED

HANDS
CUT IN
THROUGH
IMPACT

CLUB FACE OPEN

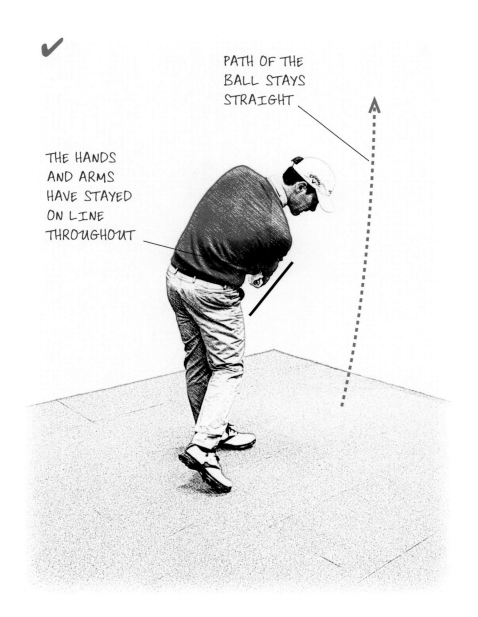

PATH OF THE
BALL STAYS
STRAIGHT

THE HANDS
AND ARMS
HAVE STAYED
ON LINE
THROUGHOUT

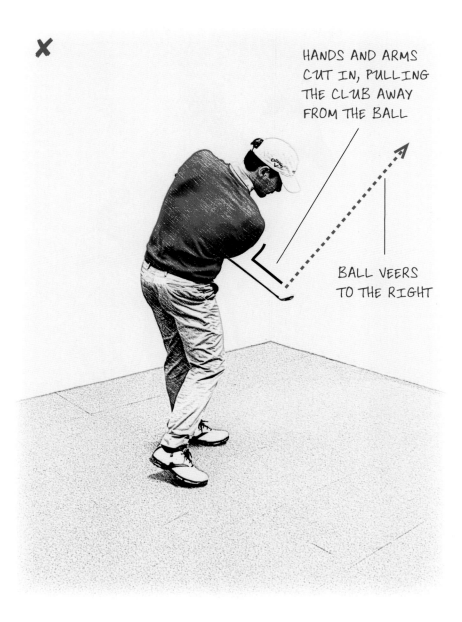

HANDS AND ARMS
CUT IN, PULLING
THE CLUB AWAY
FROM THE BALL

BALL VEERS
TO THE RIGHT

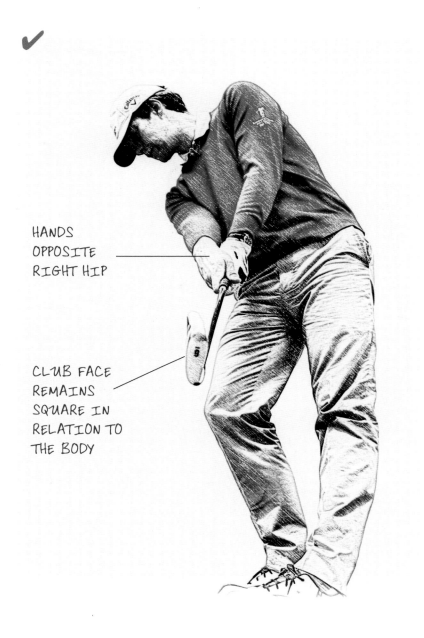

HANDS OPPOSITE RIGHT HIP

CLUB FACE REMAINS SQUARE IN RELATION TO THE BODY

HANDS HAVE
PULLED IN
ACROSS
THE BODY

CLUB FACE OPEN
THROUGH IMPACT

Another angle, clearly demonstrating how the club is
being pulled away from its intended arc.

ELBOWS CLOSE
TOGETHER

HANDS STILL
VISIBLE

CLUB HEAD
MAINTAINS
ITS ARC

✗

LEFT ELBOW PULLED AWAY INTO
A CLASSIC CHICKEN WING

HANDS HAVE
DISAPPEARED
FROM VIEW

CLUB HEAD
PULLED AWAY
FROM ITS
INTENDED ARC

This angle clearly shows how the hands have pulled in,
pushing the left elbow up and pulling the club away from
its arc through impact.

SWING THE
CLUB THROUGH
TO HIP HEIGHT

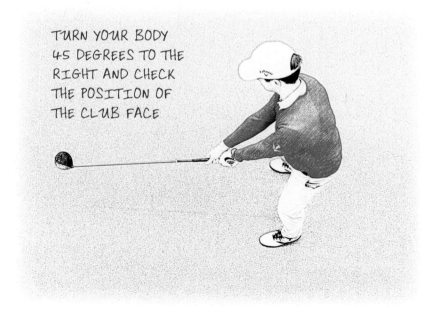

TURN YOUR BODY
45 DEGREES TO THE
RIGHT AND CHECK
THE POSITION OF
THE CLUB FACE

NOW DROP THE CLUB
TO THE GROUND.
YOU ARE NOW BACK
TO WHERE YOU
STARTED AT THE
ADDRESS, WITH THE
CLUB FACE SQUARE

Throughout the book you'll continually see references to the blade being square in relation to the body. The simple exercise on these two pages shows you what we mean by this phrase.

Later in the book, we will look at a backswing arms-in-front drill (see pages 126–129). Once that has been mastered, you can then check that the blade is square on the backswing in the same way that is shown here at the finish.

Front End Therapy

The idea of starting at the finish – or, at least, learning the golf swing back to front – may still seem illogical. Traditional instruction starts at address and the takeaway. There is, though, another way.

Front End Therapy

Now that you understand and appreciate how important the post-impact swing arc is, we can get to work on Leslie King's trademark Front End Therapy. The drill has its origins in golf's black-and-white days, before modern visual technology changed the way golfers could study their swings.

Until the introduction of the video camera, pupils often refused to accept how poor their swings were and remained reluctant to change what they felt were perfectly poised backswings and professional-looking downswings. Mr King understood this, appreciating how difficult backswing changes could be and how awkward they felt.

He therefore devised Front End Therapy. It was the first thing he built for his pupils, and they would practise it for a six-week period while retaining their old backswing. Perfecting the arc through impact compensated – to a certain extent at least – for their backswing and downswing deficiencies.

Once he was satisfied that the finish was ingrained and automatic, Mr King would reshape the rest of the swing, knowing that the finish had already brought a great improvement to a player's game.

He built thousands of swings in this way and achieved outstanding, consistent results. Juli Inkster, already a two-time US Amateur Champion when she first visited the school, embraced the drill. Michael Bonallack, Britain's greatest ever amateur, rebuilt his swing through the finish and went on to add three further consecutive Amateur Championships to the two he had already won. One young player reached the semi-final of the English Amateur Championship within eighteen months of first picking up a club, and twelve months after stepping onto a golf course for the first time. He practised exclusively in the golf school for six months before taking his game outside.

Today, the Front End Therapy drill is just as relevant and important as ever. The backswing and downswing are now generally well understood but the post-impact arc is still regarded as a mere afterthought, warranting little attention. But make no mistake – sculpting the post-impact arc can vastly improve a player's game, and perfecting Front End Therapy is essential in achieving that.

To begin with, the drill should be performed in super-slow motion, a technique that is integral to our teaching and will help you rapidly achieve total mastery and understanding of any stage of the swing. Once you feel comfortable with the new movement, your swing will begin to gain momentum and quickly evolve into a unified, free-flowing action.

Though this concept may be new to you, the process is commonplace in other high-precision sports and activities. Italian footballer Gianfranco Zola learnt to spin and shape his free kicks by practising them in slow motion, and racing driver Jackie Stewart told us that when he was at his finest he felt like he was driving in slow motion. Dancers also learn their steps and movements in this way. The legendary Michael Flatley, *Strictly Come Dancing*'s Anton Du Beke and the Royal Ballet's Matthew Golding are all students at the school and agree that learning the swing with us is very similar to the way they learnt to dance: we choreograph a swing as you would a dance. We push and pull our pupils through a series of simple movements that are learnt individually before being linked together into one smooth, free-flowing movement.

If you've not been to the school before or read any of our previous books, you may find this approach rather unusual. We agree that you won't have read this in many other golf books or magazine instruction articles. But we can assure you it really does bring outstanding results in a very short time.

For the beginner and mid- to high-handicapper, we strongly

suggest that while changing your swing you play the ball off a tee. If you are a good player or feel comfortable playing the ball off the ground, then that is fine, but when making swing changes, it is important to give yourself every possible advantage, and we have found that practising from a tee brings far more rapid improvement.

To release the club and maintain its arc, you must be able to feel the club head swing through the space occupied by the tee between the ball and the ground. This allows you to clip the ball away while making the cleanest of contacts. Try to hit the ball from the ground while learning the new movement and you will invariably crash the club into the ground, your hands and arms will cut in and jump up, and you will destroy your arc.

Once you become more familiar and confident with the technique, you should be able to drop the ball to the ground without problems. We suggest playing three or four shots off the tee, followed by one or two off the ground.

The beginner lady golfer, however, should play almost all their golf off a tee for a three- to six-month period while ingraining their fledgling swings. The male golfer can generally get away with a little more brute force to get the ball moving forwards but, for the lady, the technique needs to be a little purer. You may encounter numerous 'experts' keen to offer their advice who insist that playing off a tee is cheating. Rest assured, these people are mistaken. Once your swing is natural, flowing and strong, they will keep their opinions to themselves!

So, we are almost ready to go. Practise Front End Therapy, initially in slow motion. With constant repetition, the speed and fluidity of the swing will build and you'll be well on your way to rapid, sustained improvement.

BACK IS STRAIGHT
BUT NOT STIFF

BODY LEANS
OVER FROM
THE HIPS

THE HANDS AND
ARMS HANG
FREELY FROM
THE BODY

KNEES ARE
SLIGHTLY
FLEXED

The images over the next few pages will show you how
to keep the club on a constant arc through the finish.

CLUB SWINGS
BACK TO MIDWAY
BETWEEN THE
KNEES AND HIPS

Take your address and draw the club head back to thigh height. Make sure your wrist angles have stayed constant and your hands have stayed on their arc and not rolled (more of which later).

RIGHT KNEE
FOLDS TOWARDS
TARGET

CLUB FACE
SQUARE BEFORE
IMPACT

In slow motion, swing the club back to the ball, making sure your right knee and foot and both hips are turning into the ball. Keep your head centred.

LEFT KNEE
BEGINS TO
STRAIGHTEN

CLUB FACE
REMAINS SQUARE
AT IMPACT

Continue turning the lower body towards the target.

BLADE REMAINS
SQUARE AFTER
IMPACT

A few inches after impact, the blade remains square. The hands retain their arc and the arms retain their radius as they swing beyond the ball – do not pull them upwards or across the ball. The club shaft is an extension of this movement.

At what we term the 'quarter finish', the blade is square
in relation to the body.

THE HANDS AND
ARMS ARE IN
LINE WITH THE
RIGHT HIP

THE BLADE
REMAINS
SQUARE

The hands and arms retain their radius from the body.

AT THE THREE-
QUARTER FINISH,
THE HIPS HAVE
FULLY TURNED

THE RIGHT
FOOT IS UP
ON ITS TOE

DROP THE ARMS
BACK TO HIP
HEIGHT AND
CHECK THAT THE
CLUB FACE IS
STILL SQUARE

The finish is now complete.

G   H   I

Here is the Front End Therapy sequence in its entirety. Remember to practise this in slow motion so that you can check your position at each stage.

Once you have done this a few times, and the motion starts to feel more familiar, gradually increase the pace until you are swinging at a regular speed.

Overhead Views

As we have said, we hope this book gives you a jolt, changes your perspective and makes you rethink some of your golfing assumptions. The overhead shots are part of this idea. The chances are, you will never have seen shots played from this angle, but it clearly illustrates how even the smallest of incorrect motions can have a big impact on your overall swing. So let's give it a go – why not try to reconfigure the way you see things?

It is important to realise that, as shown in the Understanding the Arc chapter, the club face may well start off square but could still open or close a nanosecond before impact. That is why it is crucial to build a consistent arc through the finish.

The next few pages will show what happens when the club head remains square throughout the impact zone as compared to becoming open; look at the difference between the position of the hands in these sequences, as well as that of the elbows, and see what an effect it has on the position and angle of the club – and ultimately the direction in which the ball will travel.

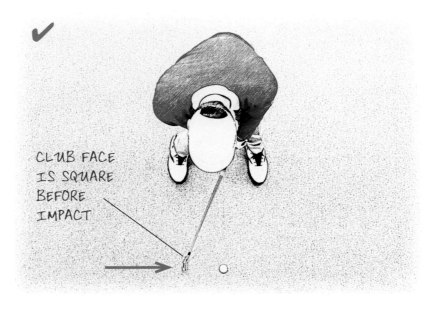

CLUB FACE IS SQUARE BEFORE IMPACT

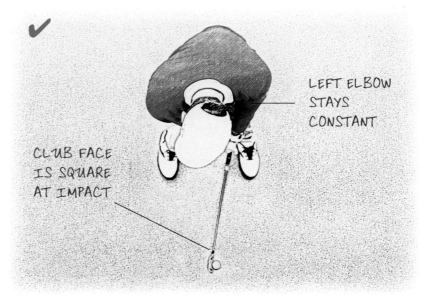

LEFT ELBOW STAYS CONSTANT

CLUB FACE IS SQUARE AT IMPACT

CLUB FACE
IS OPEN
BEFORE
IMPACT

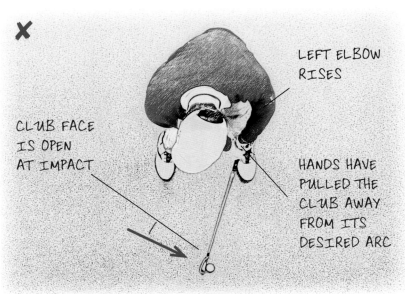

LEFT ELBOW
RISES

CLUB FACE
IS OPEN
AT IMPACT

HANDS HAVE
PULLED THE
CLUB AWAY
FROM ITS
DESIRED ARC

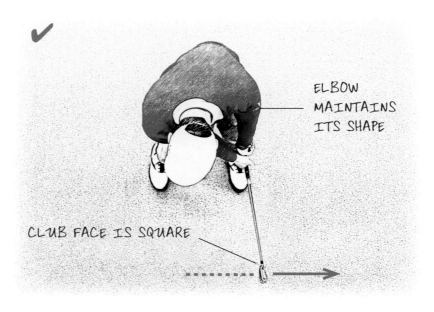

ELBOW MAINTAINS ITS SHAPE

CLUB FACE IS SQUARE

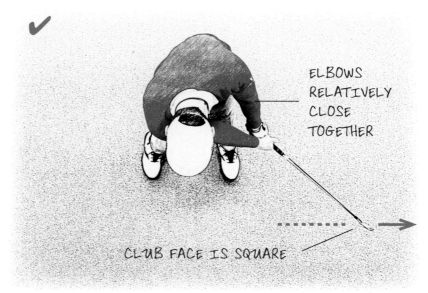

ELBOWS RELATIVELY CLOSE TOGETHER

CLUB FACE IS SQUARE

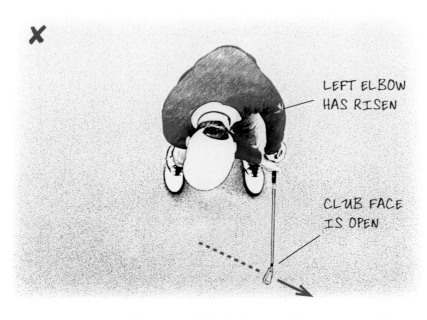

LEFT ELBOW
HAS RISEN

CLUB FACE
IS OPEN

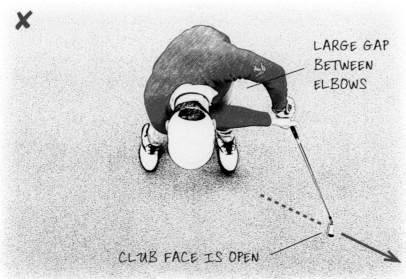

LARGE GAP
BETWEEN
ELBOWS

CLUB FACE IS OPEN

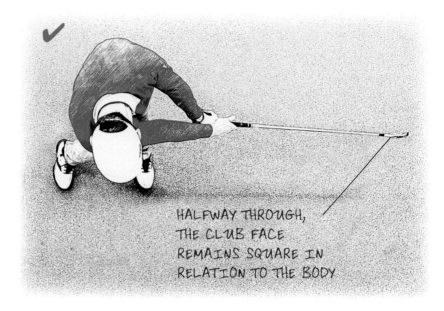

HALFWAY THROUGH,
THE CLUB FACE
REMAINS SQUARE IN
RELATION TO THE BODY

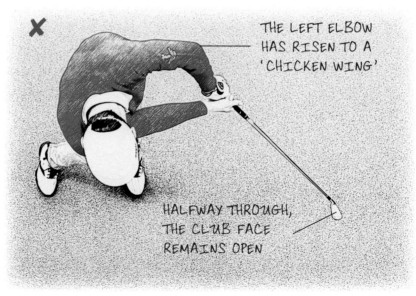

THE LEFT ELBOW
HAS RISEN TO A
'CHICKEN WING'

HALFWAY THROUGH,
THE CLUB FACE
REMAINS OPEN

The Impact Bag Drill

Every golfer knows what an impact bag is. Few, though, use it effectively. The problem is in the name – most players see the impact bag as something to smash as hard as they can.

What they do not realise is that their hands invariably jump up as they hit the bag. They come off the hand arc and lose their radius. They think the drill is all about power but it's all about placement. They think they are improving their golf swing but they are doing the exact opposite.

Impact bags were designed to allow golfers to practise placing the club head on the back of the bag so that the face is perfectly square at impact. If power is your sole focus, you are unlikely to see or feel anything at all. We recommend that you swing in slow motion when you start practising this drill, and then gradually increase the speed until you have a fluid motion. Look at your club face as it hits the bag, look at the angle of your club shaft. Look, see and feel.

Then take this lesson one stage further. Move the bag and place it outside your lead foot, nearer the target. We call this the quarter finish. Then repeat your slow-motion swing. Retain your hand arc. Make sure you have not held your hands open or rolled them over. Check if your club face is still square in relation to your body. This is crucial – the club face must not just be square to your body at impact but throughout the impact zone, before and after the ball.

The pictures on the following pages show an impact bag being struck with an open club face, a closed club face, and a correct strike with a square club face. Look at each carefully so that you can compare your own strikes.

OPEN CLUB FACE – IF THIS WERE A BALL, IT WOULD BE GOING HIGH AND RIGHT

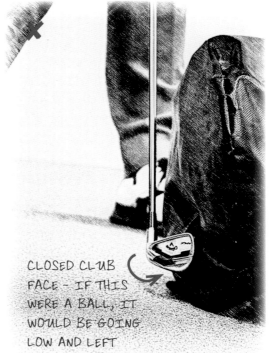

CLOSED CLUB FACE – IF THIS WERE A BALL, IT WOULD BE GOING LOW AND LEFT

These images give you a close-up view of the club head on impact: open, closed and square.

SQUARE CLUB FACE
— IF THIS WERE A BALL,
IT WOULD BE GOING
LONG AND STRAIGHT

HANDS HOLD
CLUB FACE OPEN

Impact: Club face is open

HANDS AHEAD
OF CLUB FACE

HAND HELD OPEN
THROUGH IMPACT

Quarter finish: Club face is open.

The result of this swing will be the ball heading deep into the rough/trees/ocean on the right-hand side of the fairway.

HANDS TURN OVER

Impact: Club face closed.

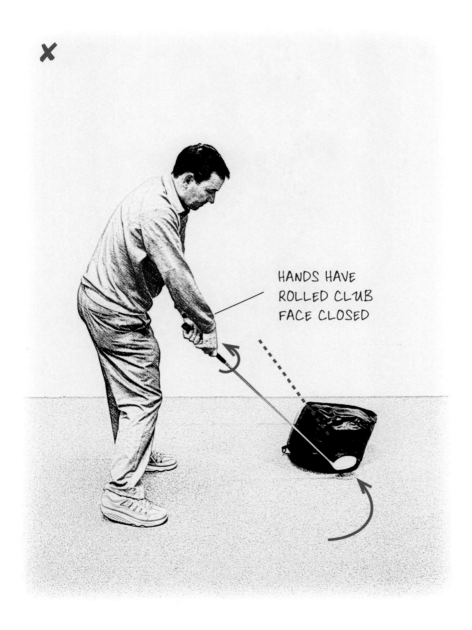

HANDS HAVE
ROLLED CLUB
FACE CLOSED

HANDS TWIST
CLUB FACE
CLOSED

Quarter finish: Club face closed.

The ball will swing to the left after this shot.

CORRECT HAND
POSITION KEEPS
CLUB HEAD
SQUARE

Impact: Club face square.

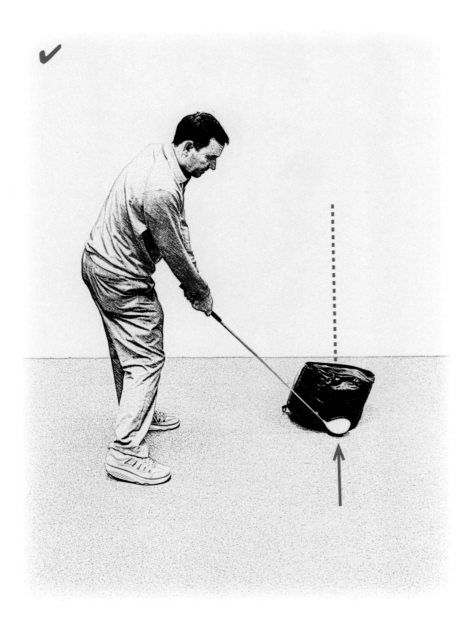

Quarter finish: Club remains square in relation to
the body.

With this shot, the ball is driven powerfully and accurately
down the middle of the fairway.

Here you can clearly compare these views of the club at impact, with the club head open (opposite, top), closed (opposite, bottom) and square (above). Make sure your impact resembles the position in the images above.

Now at the quarter finish, again
these pages instantly show you the
difference between the club face being
open (opposite, top), closed (opposite,
bottom), and square (above).

The Football Drill

Once you start to focus on the relationship of the club face and the impact bag – and the way the hands maintain their angles and the hand arc is retained – then repeat the drill with a ball. A big ball.

Again, the emphasis is on a slow-motion swing initially, to retain a sense of flow while also concentrating on how the body, hands and arms work together through the swing without worrying about power.

Our pupils often find it hard to relate to a small golf ball, but they can really see how things work with a football, to the point where they often do what is right instinctively. Everything is exaggerated with a large ball – if your hands leave their arc, for instance, you will hit further up the ball rather than hitting right at its base.

Similarly, if you cut across the ball or roll your hands, the ball will clearly tell you what has happened by the way it flies, in contrast to a motionless impact bag.

In the following sequences, you will see a ball being hit with an open, a square and a closed club face. The ball will tell the story, going right, straight or left. It is highly likely, however, that you will already be fully aware of where your club was facing at impact – you will already know, thanks to the size of the football, whether you have got it right or wrong.

CLUB FACE IS OPEN

BALL FLIES
TO THE RIGHT

CLUB FACE IS CLOSED

BALL FLIES
TO THE LEFT

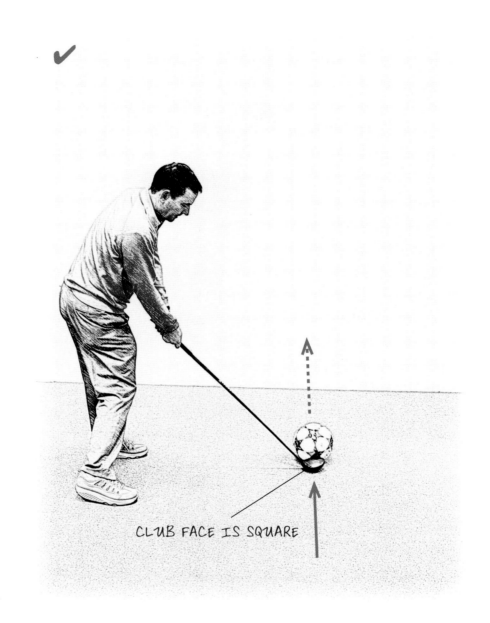

CLUB FACE IS SQUARE

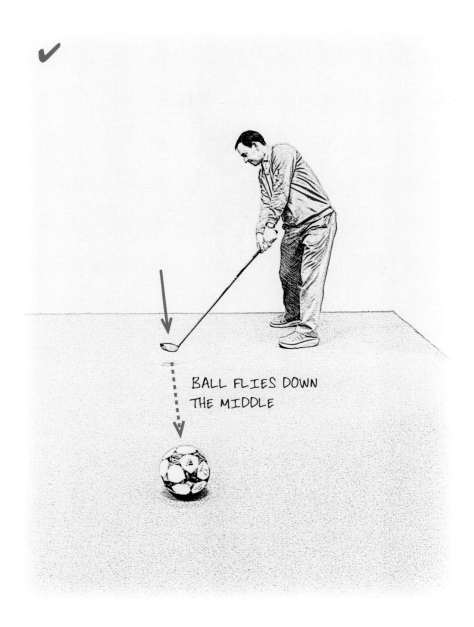

BALL FLIES DOWN
THE MIDDLE

Compare these pictures side by side to clearly see the difference of the club face and the way the hands are working just before impact.

Again, compare these pictures to see the difference in the position of the club post impact, and the effect that has had on the path of the ball.

The Backswing Problem

We have sculpted our finish and we know where our swing is heading. Now is the time to go back to the very start — the backswing — while always keeping in mind the fact that what we practise here must marry seamlessly with our new impact position and finish.

The Backswing Problem

The backswing may seem a simple action, yet every day at the school we see the same problem wrecking the start of our pupils' swings. It is caused by rolling hands. Nine out of ten golfers do it. And if you roll your hands, they will come off their arc.

Is this so critical? Yes. Is it possible to skip this segment? No. Hand roll affects the way your arms work and distorts your swing radius. Hand roll affects everything. Nine out of ten golfers have destroyed their backswing within the first few feet of the takeaway, as you can see in the pictures opposite.

We have been battling to eliminate hand roll for years, back when very few other golf instructors were addressing the problem at all. Despite all our efforts though, it remains a prominent part of our vocabulary.

These days, things have changed and people are more widely aware of the problem. The top players have great hand action. Even most high-handicap golfers are aware they should not be rolling their hands during the takeaway.

They are less sure, however, how to stop doing it. The drills in this section are designed to help with this problem.

THE HANDS HAVE
REMAINED IN
A CONSTANT
POSITION
DURING THE
TAKEAWAY

A LINE PROJECTED
FROM THE SHAFT
POINTS WELL
INSIDE THE BALL

These pictures clearly show the difference in the
backswing between keeping your hands constant (above)
and rolling your hands (opposite).

THE HANDS
HAVE TWISTED
OR ROLLED
THE CLUB

A LINE PROJECTED
FROM THE SHAFT
POINTS WELL
OUTSIDE THE BALL

THE HANDS AND
ARMS HANG
FREELY FROM
THE BODY

The following sequence will show you how to keep your
hands constant during the backswing, eliminating hand
roll. Set up at address, then go through your swing in
slow motion, paying close attention to the position of
your hands at each stage.

THE HANDS
STAY CONSTANT
AS THEY TAKE
THE CLUB
AWAY FROM
THE BALL

THE HANDS
ARE IN LINE
WITH THE
LEFT THIGH

THE WRISTS
HAVE HINGED

THE CLUB FACE IS
SQUARE OR SLIGHTLY
CLOSED

THE CLUB FACE
IS SQUARE OR
SLIGHTLY CLOSED

WRIST BREAK
CONTAINED

SHOULDERS
FULLY
TURNED

This is the final point of your backswing, the correct
position if your hands have stayed constant throughout
the motion.

The image above shows the same final position of the backswing, but using the wood instead. The swing is slightly fuller with the wood. This is simply due to the longer shaft and the club should be swung in exactly the same way.

A

B

C

D

E

The backswing sequence in full, demonstrating the constant position of the hands.

The Grip

In considering the backswing, it is also important to mention the grip. There is no right or wrong about the style of grip you choose. Harry Vardon could play a bit – he won six Opens – and he championed the grip that was named after him. Jack Nicklaus, Tiger Woods and Juli Inkster could – and can – play a bit as well, and they opted for the interlocking grip. If it works for you, it works for you.

All we suggest is that if you are struggling to make either of these classic grips work for you, then try the two-handed grip. It is the oldest grip in golf and we often see pupils adopt it and transform their games. We think it makes what we teach in the backswing a lot easier, and it makes the release of the club through the ball a lot easier too. The two-handed 'baseball' grip puts more right hand onto the club and thus gives players more control of the shaft. This helps stop hand roll and helps you release the club at impact.

If you have used another grip for years and you're happy, stick with it. If not, we strongly recommend giving the two-handed grip a go.

Whichever grip you choose, you must make sure you don't hold the club too tightly; this will make it almost impossible to release the club head into the ball. The ideal pressure is not easy to explain, but there is an old saying: you should hold the club as you would a little bird in your hands – you don't want to harm it, but you don't want it to fly away. We think this describes the feeling well.

THE SMALL FINGER OF THE RIGHT HAND SITS ON TOP AND IN BETWEEN THE FIRST AND SECOND FINGERS OF THE LEFT HAND

The overlapping Vardon grip. In all three grips, the forefinger is triggered – pointing slightly away from the middle finger. This helps maintain the correct hand line on the backswing, and helps to deliver the club head into the ball at impact.

THE SMALL FINGER
OF THE RIGHT HAND
INTERTWINES
WITH THE FIRST
AND SECOND
FINGERS OF THE
LEFT HAND

The interlocking grip.

ALL TEN FINGERS OF THE HANDS ARE PLACED ON THE CLUB

The two-handed baseball grip.

The Hand-Around-
the-Wrist Drill

If you struggle with hand roll, this is the drill for you. It's ridiculously simple and you can do it anywhere. Simply get into your address position then take your right hand off the club and grip your left wrist with it, squeezing it so your thumb and fingers meet.

Now swing back with the left arm. The right hand holding the left wrist will encourage you not to roll your hands. Look at the back of your left hand as you swing back – it will not twist or roll or bow. The slightly concave angle at the back of the left hand (if you have a neutral grip) remains the same, and your left hand stays on its arc.

The final picture of the sequence in the following pages shows the club shaft running along the left forearm. This is an exaggerated position – ideally, the shaft would be slightly less upright and on a shallower angle, running along the inside of the right forearm or bicep. We have exaggerated it to emphasise the point – hand rollers would at this point have the shaft below the right forearm, or even horizontal to the ground. Exaggerating this position will help you make the change from your previously ingrained, destructive shaft position.

Grip the club with the left hand. Hold the left wrist with
the right hand, squeezing the fingers and thumb together.

Start to swing the club back with the left hand.

Maintaining a firm grip on your wrist, continue to swing the club, taking it up to hip height.

The shaft should now be in line with the left arm in an exaggerated 'good' position.

The Split-Hand Drill

The split-hand drill is similar to the hand-around-the-wrist drill, but emphasises the correct wrist feelings in a different way.

Hold the club normally in both hands but then let the right one drop down the grip so that there are two or three inches between your hands. Now continue with a normal takeaway, focusing on retaining the same angle throughout at the back of your left wrist and keeping your hands on their arc all the way to hip level.

Splitting the hands in this way means you have more of your right hand on the club. This offers more support and fights any tendency to twist or roll the wrists. Again, the final picture of the following sequence shows an exaggeratedly upright club shaft, running along the left forearm, to help eliminate the ingrained feelings caused by hand rolling. Ideally, the shaft at this point would be a bit flatter, running along the inside of the right forearm or bicep.

Grip the club with the right hand two to three inches below the left.

Take the club away while maintaining the angle of the hands and arms.

At hip height the shaft runs down the left arm – again, an exaggerated position, more upright than necessary and designed to help eliminate the dreaded rolling of the hands.

The Arms-in-Front Drill

If there is a signature Leslie King drill, then this has to be it. It's so simple yet so good for improving golf swings! As with the previous two drills, it's great for reinforcing the perfect halfway back position, while also promoting the feelings of correct hand action.

Take your address position. Now raise your arms directly in front of you, retaining your body position and without changing your wrist angles until the club head is around waist-high.

Now turn your shoulders to the right, without moving your head and, again, without twisting or rolling the wrists. You should be in the perfect halfway back position.

Set up at address.

Keep your body down while lifting the hands and arms
in front of you.

Turn your upper body to the right, maintaining the angle of the wrists and hands. The shaft runs down the right bicep. Now you can check that the blade is still square in relation to the body by repeating the exercise from pages 42–43.

Downswing and Release

Contrary to what you may have been led to believe, releasing the club too early on the downswing is not a problem for the average golfer. It is actually releasing the club too late that is a huge problem for struggling players.

Downswing and Release

When we first started teaching back in the 1970s, a huge majority of golfers started the downswing by turning the shoulders. This threw the club outside the ideal downswing path and across the ball, resulting in pulls, slices and all manner of wayward shots.

These days we more frequently see the very opposite – and potentially more damaging – problem. Players are so fixated with bringing the club down on an inside path that they are totally blocked and stuck as they enter the impact area.

Once in this position, their only option is to pull their hands and arms up and away from the ball just before or after impact – the very thing that this book is designed to eliminate.

The obsession with trying to hit late is also a huge problem, causing more trouble. This is more damaging to the struggling golfer than anything else. The mis-hit shots of the talented Tour professional may indeed be caused by an early release of the club, but the struggler hardly releases the club at all.

With all the instruction you've seen and read, you may find this a little hard to believe. We can assure you that this is a fact.

At the school we have videos of more than 12,000 golfers on our iPads. You would struggle to find more than a handful who suffer from releasing the club too early. The club head can be turned or flipped over but this is a different problem, illustrated in the drills in this chapter and in Front End Therapy.

At the top of the backswing the body is perfectly poised in anticipation of starting the downswing. From here, that should be quite straightforward, as the hands and arms simply swing the club back down on the same path as they've just come up.

The downswing is felt through a fluidity of movement in the hands and wrists. The hips move laterally to the left. At this stage they essentially should be in the same position as at address.

The hips now begin to turn; the right hand begins to release the club into the ball.

The right hand continues to square the club face.

A few inches before impact, the club face is square.

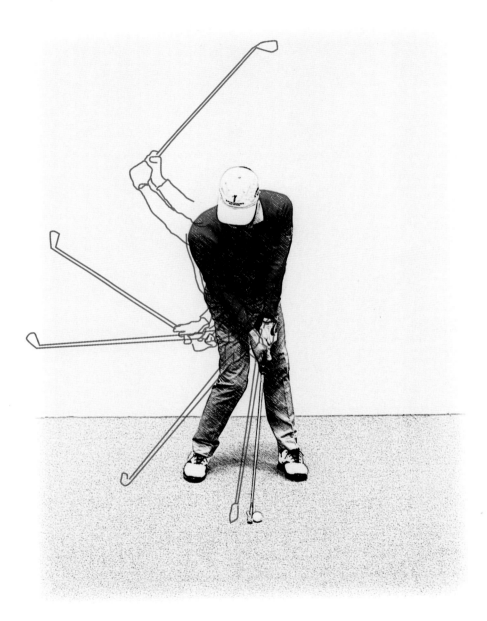

At impact, the club face is still square. If you attempt to pull the club down from the top of the backswing and hit late, your chances of achieving this are remote.

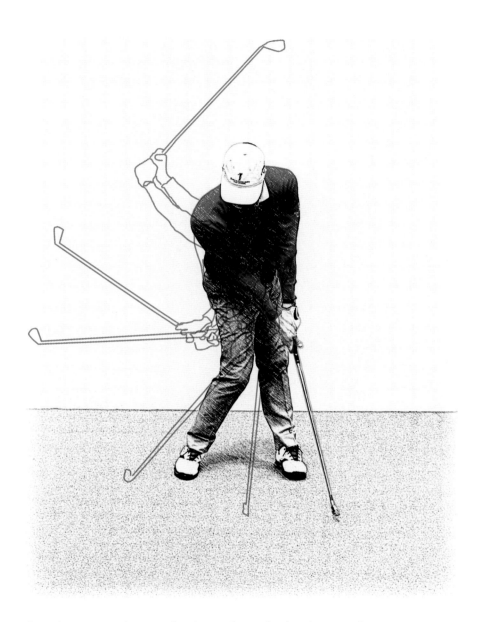

Post impact, we're now back to where the book started. The blade is still square, the hands have stayed on the inner wheel, and the club has stayed on the outer wheel.

Now well into the finish, both the hands and arms have retained their radius throughout the impact zone. The next pages show the sequence in full.

A

B

E

F

C

D

G

H

Tennis Racket Drills

Using a tennis racket, with its large head, allows you to relate better to what your club face is doing throughout the swing. Many golfers can overlook how important club-face angles are when using a golf club and can get sidetracked in their search for power rather than precision.

Set yourself up side on to a wall. Leave about two or three feet between you and the wall, so that you will just touch it as you extend your arms in the throughswing.

Hold the racket in your right hand, with the left one hanging down by your side. Now carry out slow-motion swings. If you swing correctly, and release the racket through impact, the tip of the head will come into contact with the wall.

If you hold your hand open, however, you will not release the racket and the bottom edge of the head will strike the wall. If you roll your hand over, you will flip the racket rather than release it correctly and the top edge will meet with the wall.

Hold the tennis racket in the right hand, with the left by
your side.

Swing the racket back and release it through. The tip hits the wall first.

Holding the hand open creates an open face – the bottom of the racket will hit the wall first.

If your hand turns over as you swing, creating a closed
face, the top edge of the racket strikes the wall.

Now carry out the same exercise, but with two hands on the racket. Do not tighten your grip. Many players do just that with their left hand at this point, which blocks the release.

Using two hands to practise this drill will allow you to monitor if you are making this mistake when you go out on the course.

The Net Drill

The net drill is very similar to the one using the tennis racket, but with a net (or a sheet hanging from a washing line) in front of you, and this time you will be able to use one of your clubs. Perhaps start with a large-headed club such as a driver, to ensure you keep focusing on the face angle.

Go through the same procedure as with the tennis racket drill but concentrate hard on your hand action, on your club head and on the relationship between the two. The large-headed racket is easier to see but you will quickly get used to seeing how the angle of the golf club face can be radically affected by limited hand action. Keep practising until you build up the feel of a correct hand and club release.

Set up at address – remember not to hold the club too
tightly with the left hand.

Swing the club freely back and through into the net.
Keep the club face square in relation to the body.

If the club face is held open it will block the release and send the ball high to the right.

Rolling hands will send the ball low and left.

Back to the Finish

This book began back to front, starting with the finish. We stressed the importance of hand arc, swing radius and correct hand action. We moulded the movement in slow motion. We then returned to the start in order to examine the takeaway, backswing and release. We now find ourselves back at our pre-sculpted finish, ready to sew these different elements together.

Back to the Finish

In these pages we will omit the wrong way to carry out the finish, concentrating solely on the right method, and we will shift perspective yet again by scrutinising the action from an angle rarely illustrated in books or videos.

Look at the sequence in the following pages and you will now appreciate the simplicity and clean lines of this finish. Focus on the hands and their total lack of twisting or rolling. Imagine the hand arc. Focus on the club face and the way it remains square to the body throughout. Look at the body poise and the maintaining of angles and correct posture. Having got to the finish, our golfer then allows his hands to drop back down to hip level.

The shaft is now in front of him, at a 45-degree angle to the ground, as he watches the flight of his shot. At this point, he also checks that the face of the club has remained square in relation to his body. The leading edge of the club face is vertical – that spells a straight shot. Any deviation would suggest that the club head has been held open or rolled over at some stage during the swing – a leading edge off the vertical to the left would mean a closed club face and a pull or hook, an edge off to the right an open club face and a push or slice.

RIGHT KNEE
FOLDS IN
TOWARDS
LEFT KNEE

LEFT KNEE
BEGINS TO
STRAIGHTEN

CLUB FACE IS SQUARE SIX
INCHES BEFORE IMPACT

HIPS TURNED
OPEN 45
DEGREES TO
THE TARGET

LEFT KNEE
CONTINUES TO
STRAIGHTEN

BALL STRUCK WITH THE
MIDDLE OF THE CLUB FACE

HIPS
CONTINUE
TO TURN

HANDS
MAINTAIN
THEIR
RADIUS

CLUB FACE IS SQUARE IN
RELATION TO THE BODY

HANDS
FOLLOW
THEIR ARC
AND ARE
STILL
VISIBLE AS
THEY RETAIN
THEIR
RADIUS

HANDS STILL
VISIBLE

RIGHT KNEE
AND FOOT
FOLD IN
TOWARDS
THE TARGET

HANDS NOW
DISAPPEAR
FROM VIEW

SHAFT REAPPEARS
OUTSIDE THE
LEFT SHOULDER

LEFT LEG
IS NOW
ALMOST
COMPLETELY
STRAIGHT

HIP TURN
IS ALMOST
COMPLETE

RIGHT FOOT
IS UP ON
BIG TOE

THE HIPS
HAVE TURNED
90 DEGREES

THE RIGHT
KNEE TOUCHES
THE LEFT,
WHICH IS
COMPLETELY
STRAIGHT

ARMS BACK
TO HIP
HEIGHT

Once the swing is complete, drop the arms to hip height, and check the angle of the club face. Hold this position until the ball comes to rest.

A   B   C

D   E   F

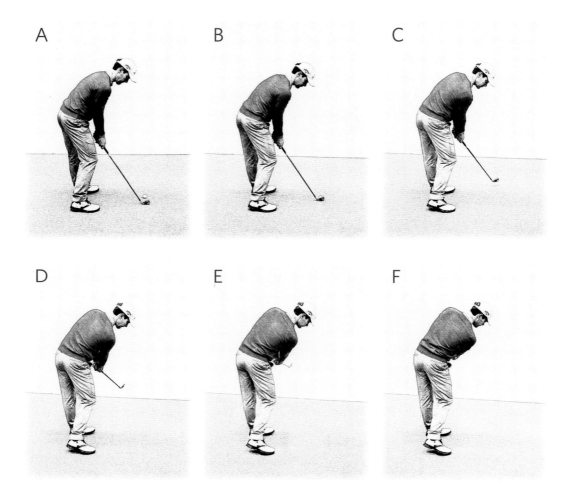

G

H

I

J

Looking at the entire sequence of pictures together, you can see how smooth your movements through to the finish should appear.

Overhead Views

Golf instruction rarely looks at the swing from overhead. To us, however, it makes perfect sense. You may never see other golfers – let alone yourself – from above, but new perspectives invariably inspire new thoughts and understanding.

Look at the following images which show both an open and square club face a few inches before impact and at the moment of impact itself. As well as looking at the club head, also examine the shoulder and the left arm from this angle. The open-club-face pictures offer a clear view of the dreaded chicken wing, which will throttle the release of the club, thus leaking power and strangling the finish.

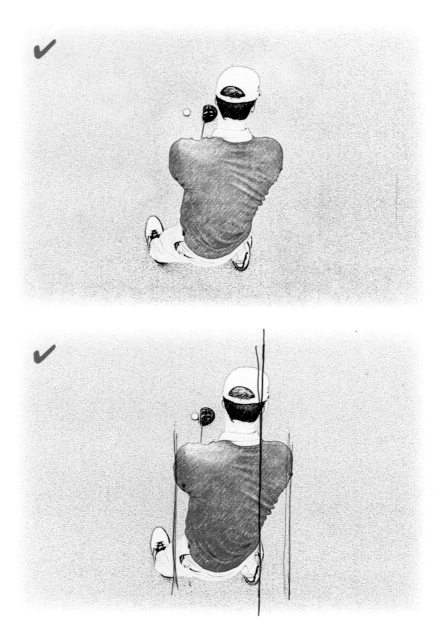

Club head square before and at impact. The left arm points straight down. This shot is going right down the middle of the fairway.

Club face open before and at impact. The left shoulder is rising and the left arm is pulling away from the chest and breaking at the elbow. This ball is heading way right and will fall short.

Club face square (continued).

Club face open (continued).

In the top picture you can see the club has remained square, whereas in the bottom one it is still open, and the left elbow has risen.

The Connected Drill

'Connection' is a word that often crops up in golf instruction, but it is not always well understood. This drill, however, is particularly valuable since it not only helps maintain the correct connection between the arms and body during the golf swing, but it also connects the key lessons we have been illustrating in this book.

Take a driver and grip it halfway down the shaft, with the butt touching your belly button. Take the club away in slow motion to just under waist height – there is no breaking of the wrists – then return to impact and into the half finish, all the time ensuring the butt does not lose contact with your abdomen.

Retain this connection and you will have maintained your hands on the hand arc. Your radius will have remained the same. There will have been no hand roll. And the arms and body will be working together in unison. This drill truly is a catch-all.

Grip the driver – the end of the shaft meets the belly button.

Keep the contact with your midriff — if you lose it, you
are probably a hand roller!

Swing back down in slow motion.

Complete the action to hip height, retaining the connection throughout. Look at how the club face has remained square to the body.

The Arms-in-Front Drill

This arms-in-front drill is the mirror image of the one illustrated earlier (see pages 126–129), and another of Leslie King's favourites. The previous one was designed to give the feel of the perfect halfway back position. This one does the same but for the halfway through position. It isolates a key moment on the way to a perfect finish.

Repeat this drill regularly. It will act as a constant reminder that the hands should retain the same angle that was set at address, allowing the club face to remain square throughout.

The turning of the hips and the movement of the right knee and foot also underline that the body must not stall or stop turning through the impact zone. Everything works in unison. Stop turning and you will either chicken-wing or resort to rolling your hands over in a last-gasp attempt to square the club face.

Take your address.

Keeping the body down, lift the arms in front of you.

Turn to the left and allow the right knee and foot to fold towards the left knee, so that it ends up parallel to the target line. The club face is square to the body.

Alternative Finishes, Alternative Swings

Golfers and their swings come in all shapes and sizes. There is no identikit golf swing, nor should there be. We work around each individual in sculpting their actions and there are certain variations on the finish that you may find work just as well.

Alternative Finishes, Alternative Swings

Now that you fully understand the structure of the finish and have learnt how to swing the club correctly into pre-impact, we can begin to shape the ball right or left by making slight adjustments just before impact and into the follow-through.

In each of our three examples the blade is square to the target as it approaches the ball. It is now, in the split second before impact, that the blade can be softly held off to fade the ball to the right, softly turned in to draw the ball left or kept square to hit the ball straight.

You will see the professionals playing these shots frequently as they navigate their way around the golf course and you should quite easily be able to add this skill to your armoury.

You will see the held-off open blade employed as a standard technique by many of the world's top players, past and present – and most noticeably today by Jordan Spieth.

These players play off a slightly closed backswing blade angle and hold the blade open pre-impact and into the follow-through.

Many think that Spieth's high left elbow is similar to the dreaded chicken wing that we highlight throughout this book, but we can assure you that it's not. The arc and radius are maintained perfectly as the blade is held open to compensate for the closed blade of the backswing. In the chicken wing, the hands pull in and the left elbow rises and is pulled across the body, destroying the arc of the club through impact and beyond.

The naturally gifted player who constantly repeats this action enjoys great results with this technique and we would never advocate changing a slightly unconventional swing that repeats itself consistently. We always work within a player's own individual mannerisms.

This brings us nicely onto the subject of 'method' and gives us the opportunity to clear up a few widely held misconceptions.

Every few weeks, a tired old picture turns up on social

media showing great players with unconventional backswings, accompanied by text suggesting that you can swing the club back any way you like and still be great at golf. Teachers, it is argued, shouldn't teach particular methods since there are clearly so many ways to swing the club effectively. This is very true in the case of fabulously talented golfers, but completely misleading when applied to lesser, long-suffering players.

Every good player with an unconventional backswing naturally compensates for it on the way down, through impact and beyond. Jim Furyk is a classic example. His backswing may look unorthodox, but immediately he brings the club down and through the ball he is in exactly the same position as the greatest players of his, and any other, generation.

For struggling golfers, it is a very different story. They cannot compensate to a sufficient degree to allow for severely flawed fundamentals. For them, the easiest and quickest solution is to clean up the whole swing.

The simple fact is that you need a structured swing model as a blueprint to be able to work with all types of swing variations. The beauty of having a swing model is that it takes you from A to Z in the simplest of ways, but we would never dream of overhauling an effective action just because it doesn't match our model – that would make absolutely no sense at all.

Having a structured model is also the only way that those lacking natural ability can be taught to play an acceptable, enjoyable standard of golf. They can be pushed and pulled through the swing and, with constant practice and repetition, achieve outstanding results.

Examine the swing sequences on the following pages. At the start, the player's swing looks identical in each picture, to the naked eye at least, although he himself would be able to feel minute differences in each case. The minor adjustments he is introducing, however, become ever clearer from page 200 onwards.

FADE DRAW

A few inches before impact, the club face is square. At this point, the three pictures on these pages are practically identical. However, in each sequence on the following pages you are about to see a barely visible variation introduced that, as the swing progresses, will have a very visible impact on the final stages of the swing – and the path of the ball.

STRAIGHT

FADE

DRAW

It is still difficult to see the differences at this stage, but on the left, the hands hold the club face fractionally open; in the middle picture, the hands turn the club face slightly closed; and to the right, the hands are holding the club face square at impact.

STRAIGHT

FADE

DRAW

Post impact, and the difference is becoming more discernible now: on the left the club face is open; in the middle it is closed; and to the right the club face is square. Look also at the position of his hands in relation to his body and the hand action itself. Even the head is positioned slightly differently, and the body poise shows small variations.

STRAIGHT

FADE DRAW

At the quarter finish the differences are now much more obvious. Look at the position of the hands in each and the effect that has on the club face: it is held open on the left; it is closing in the middle; and it remains perfectly square in relation to the body on the right.

STRAIGHT

FADE

DRAW

By the time the shaft approaches the horizontal in the finish, the differences are clear. The biggest clue as to where these shots are heading is provided by the club face. The swing on the left, where the club face is open, will promote a fade; the one in the middle, where the club face is closed, a draw; and the one on the right, with the club face square, an arrow-straight ball flight.

The fade shot has been slightly held off by the hands and the left elbow. This is not a chicken wing but it puts the slightest of brakes on the release of the shaft. Similarly, the elbow in the draw shot is tucked slightly further in, allowing for a more vigorous release. The variations in the shape of the elbow become more pronounced in the following pages.

STRAIGHT

FADE

LEFT ELBOW
SLIGHTLY OUT

DRAW

HANDS LEAN OVER
TO THE LEFT

LEFT ELBOW
CLOSE TO
BODY

The position of the elbow and of the golf club now clearly show the variations in the swing in all three pictures.

STRAIGHT

LEFT ELBOW
CLOSE TO BODY

FADE

DRAW

And at the end of the finish, again you can clearly see the different positions with the face of the club held open (left); closed (middle); and square (right).

All three shots will produce good but slightly different results – the fade will move fractionally to the right and the draw will move slightly to the left, perhaps to go around an obstacle or to counter a crosswind. All three, however, despite the variations in their ball flight, should end up near the flag.

STRAIGHT

FADE

DRAW

As the club comes back down to hip height, check the club face – you can tell by the leading edge which shot has faded, drawn or travelled straight.

STRAIGHT

Conclusion

Conclusion

To most players, learning the correct post-impact arc and finish first might seem a little strange, even nonsensical. When we set to work on a player's finish we are frequently asked why we are bothering, as the ball has already left the club face.

Having enrolled in Finishing School we hope that by now you, the reader, will be able to answer that question for us, and that you are already seeing the benefits of focusing on the finish first in your own game. But let's recap once more the essential message that we are trying to convey in this book.

The finish is not an afterthought and it doesn't just happen. It must be understood, learnt and practised as much as any other area of the swing. A sound, technically correct finish is the bookend that holds together everything that has gone before.

Within the space of a round, what happens a moment before or after impact can have a huge effect on your game. It explains the appalling inconsistency each and every struggling golfer experiences; they have literally no idea as to what will happen from one shot to the next.

As we have already pointed out, there are lots of different ways to swing a club and the most unusual of swings can produce the most wonderful results.

However, what is consistently true is that no matter what individual backswing mannerisms and subsequent downswing compensations a player makes in the split second before and after impact, in order to hit the ball straight each and every great player maintains the swing's radius through the impact zone, with the club face square and travelling at the correct height.

Understanding and perfecting this most neglected stage of the golf swing is essential for every golfer, regardless of age or ability.

For the long-term struggler, the easiest and quickest way to improve your game is to work through the entire book, cleaning up each and every stage of the swing. Mastery of one particular swing stage will make each subsequent one much easier.

If you are a fairly competent striker of the ball and are happy with your fundamentals, focusing on the finish and sculpting a pure post-impact arc could be the missing piece in your swing puzzle.

Good, strong low-handicap players are likely to already possess a structured post-impact arc — it is partly what has made them the player they are. But their occasional wayward strikes and mishits are probably also caused by an imperfect movement of the club head in the nanoseconds before and after impact.

Experience has taught us that, whatever your standard of golf, building and establishing a solid pre- and post-impact arc is essential for long-term sustained improvement. It has transformed the game of tens of thousands of our pupils over the last sixty-five years and we are convinced it can do the same for you.

65 Years of the Knightsbridge Golf School

65 Years of the Knightsbridge Golf School

If the definition of pioneer is someone ahead of his or her time, then Leslie King, the founder of the Knightsbridge Golf School, was a pioneer several times over. He was among the first golf teachers to systematically study the game and develop a clear method to teach it.

Back in the 1920s, when King was a young club professional, people learnt golf by trying to copy the best players of the day. There was little point, however, in asking those same players what they were doing. Few of them really knew – this, after all, was before the advent of video. And in any case, they all seemed to have different swings.

King's response was to get on his motorbike and travel

Juli Inkster with Leslie King in the early 1980s during one of her annual trips to London.

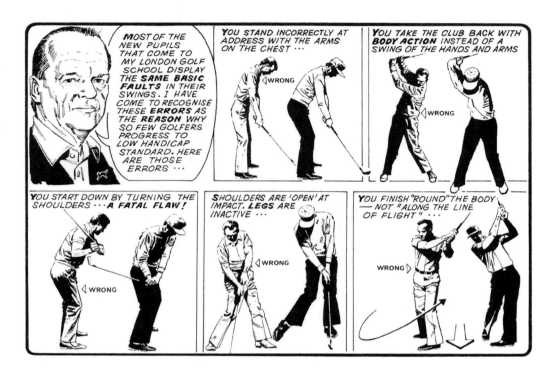

A pamphlet from the early seventies advertising Leslie King's self-published loose-leaf instruction work The Swing. Mr King insisted that nine out of ten golfers made the same mistakes; the same can be said today, although modern golfers generally have different faults to those shown here.

far and wide around the UK, attending golf tournaments and watching, watching and watching. Relying on his sharp eyesight and analytical ability, he scrutinised successful golf swings, mentally broke them down into pieces and then rebuilt them to see how they really worked. As he did so, he found common denominators. He established rules. He created a framework.

And then he went indoors. If people thought King eccentric in his desire to decode the golf swing, they must have thought him completely mad when, in 1951, he set up the Knightsbridge Golf School in a collection of disused squash courts in a basement in the heart of London.

'If you can't see where the ball has gone, how can you diagnose what your pupils have done wrong?' was a common, rather mocking reaction.

By then, however, King was familiar enough with the sport that he only had to look at the fundamentals of each golf swing to work out where the ball would end up. Not only could he do without a golf range, he could also succeed without a telephone. The school's only advertising was carried out through word of mouth – as it is still done today.

Over the years, many players have been drawn to the school. It has probably staged more lessons than any other golf centre in the world. Beginners and hackers have come seeking answers, as have Ryder and Walker Cup players, Solheim and Curtis Cup stars, amateur champions and national champions too. Some, like five-time English amateur champion Sir Michael Bonallack and seven-time Major winner Juli Inkster, went on to make it to the World Hall of Fame.

Renowned instructors also headed to the centre of London to see what all the fuss was about. David Leadbetter visited, prior to his groundbreaking work with Nick Faldo, as did Gary Player, while the great American Bob Toski would later call King 'the godfather of the modern golf swing'. Other well-known faces have also passed through the doors, such as Sean Connery, who came to the school to take some lessons in preparation for his role in *Goldfinger*.

We both started working at the school in the 1970s and since then we have been constantly developing and evolving Leslie King's original teachings into the simple and easy-to-learn swing model that we have today.

We have enjoyed success teaching on tour, and our list

Not previously a golfer, Sean Connery visited the school in preparation for his epic battle with the notorious Goldfinger.

Top: Almost all our instruction takes place in the original teaching room.
Bottom: Pupils move onto the simulators to refine their game once we are
happy with their swing.

of pupils reads like a who's who of the stage, screen and sporting worlds, though we must stress that 99 per cent of our pupils are the average player you'd find on any golf course or driving range.

In 2005, our first book had the distinction of appearing on the *Sunday Times* bestseller list, virtually unheard of for a golf instruction book. Our next two books quickly sold out their print run and second-hand copies are in high demand, although e-book editions are available.

Almost all our coaching takes place in the original teaching room; once we are happy with a pupil's swing, we progress to the simulator room to fine-tune their shotmaking.

A lot has changed at the school over the past sixty-five years; a lot, however, has remained the same. Most importantly, the core of Leslie King's instruction method remains intact. The power of word of mouth is still key in bringing new pupils through the door, and the appeal and reputation of the Knightsbridge Golf School is stronger than ever.

'At the top, I picture my perfect finish position.
My only goal on the downswing is to get there.'

Adam Scott, *Golf Monthly*, May 2016